Praying with the first Christians

Juliette Levivier

Illustrations by Anne Gravier

CTS Children's Books

Table of Contents

Jesus sends his disciples 4

The first Christians 6

St John 8

St Paul 10

St Barnabas 12

St Philip 14

St Luke 16

The martyrs, our elder brothers and sisters in the faith 18

St Stephen 20

St Tarcisius 22

St Blandina 24

St Felicity and St Perpetua. 26

The martyrs of Abitina. 28

The saints, our friends in heaven. 30

St Anthony of the Desert. 32

St Helen. 34

St Monica 36

St Augustine. 38

St Jerome 40

St Martin 42

St Nicholas 44

Jesus sends his disciples

For three years, Jesus proclaimed the Good News of the Kingdom to all those he met. He spoke of God's love and mercy and he taught his friends to do the same.

After his resurrection, Jesus appeared to his disciples. What joy for them! Jesus was alive! He said to them: "Just as the Father sent me, so I send you" (John 20:21).

A few days later, he spoke to them for the last time. "You will receive the strength of the Holy Spirit who will descend upon you. So you will be my witnesses... to the ends of the earth" (Acts 1:8).

He had hardly finished speaking, when he was taken up to heaven. A big cloud hid him from the astonished disciples! **This was the Ascension.**

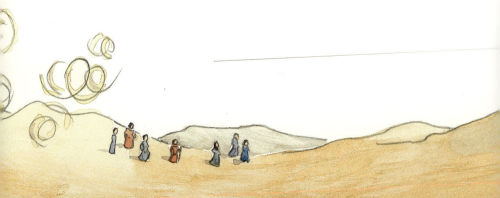

A little later, as they were gathered together in the upper room, a great noise frightened them. They saw small flames that came and rested on each of them! "They were all filled with the Holy Spirit" (Acts 2:4).

As he had promised, Jesus sent them his strength so that they too could announce the Good News to all men. **This was Pentecost.**

From then on, they did not stop proclaiming the Good News: Jesus, the Son of God, had died and risen from the dead. He is the one God sent to save all men from death and sin!

The first Christians

Many people were touched by the teaching of the Apostles and asked to be baptised. They lived joyfully, shared what they owned, prayed with one heart and listened attentively to what the Apostles had to say.

In Jerusalem, the city where Jesus suffered, died and rose again, the first Christian community was born. It would be from there that the Apostles would go to announce the Gospel throughout the whole world.

A few months later, in a city called "Antioch, for the first time, the disciples of Christ received the name 'Christians'" (Acts 11:26).

This name, 'Christian', is today still given to all those who believe that Jesus, the Christ, is the Son of God and that he has come to bring us life.

Thank you, Lord,
for all those who speak to me about you:
my parents, my catechists,
my parish priest...
I am happy to be a Christian.
I too want to announce your wonders
to those I meet.
I too want to proclaim the Good News!

St John

John lived close to Jesus and listened to his word. For a long time, he kept it inside him, thought about it and then decided to write it down.

That morning, sitting in front of his table, he finished his account. "These events have been put into writing, so that you may believe that Jesus is the Christ, the Son of God, and so that by believing you might have life in his name" (John 20:31).

He put his pen down and shut his eyes. He wanted everyone to know just how much God loves them...

Quite often, Jesus told him: "God is love", "Remain in my love." If only John, could spread this love so that all could believe!

Jesus tells me who God is, he leads me to God. Do I really believe in his love?

I too, Lord,
want to live close to you.
I want to welcome your love,
to be fruitful throughout my life.
To give fruits of joy, peace,
love and life!

St Paul

Saul was walking towards Damascus where he wanted to arrest the Christians: he hated them!

But something amazing happened on the way. All of a sudden, a bright light dazzled him. He fell to the ground and heard a voice saying to him: "Saul, Saul, why do you persecute me?" "Who are you, Lord?" asked Paul, terrified. "I am Jesus, the one you are persecuting" (Acts 9:4-5).

After praying for a long time, Saul received a visit from Ananias, a disciple of Jesus who baptised him: from then on, he was called Paul. He lived only for Jesus. He made many journeys to make Jesus known to all men.

Like Paul, Jesus calls me to change my heart so that I can share his love.

You are close to me, Lord,
but sometimes I cannot see you!
Open my eyes so that I can see you.
Open my mouth so that I can speak of you.
Open my hands so that I can serve you.
Open my heart so that I can love you.

St Barnabas

For a long time Paul had a bad reputation among the Christians. After persecuting Jesus' disciples, he was converted on the road to Damascus and then tried to show the Christian community in Jerusalem that he had really changed!

Most of Jesus' friends were suspicious but Barnabas understood that Paul really had changed. He was the one who convinced his Christian friends to trust Paul.

"Barnabas took Paul with him and introduced him to the Apostles" (Acts 9:27).

It is hard to trust. I do not always trust God and others. But without trust, I know, there is no real love.

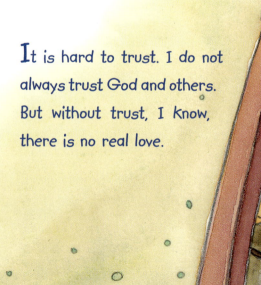

Like Barnabas, Lord,
I want to believe that we can change!
Teach me to trust.
Show me what hope is.
Make my heart big enough
to know how to welcome
those who have hurt me.

St Philip

As he was travelling, Philip met an Ethiopian who was reading the Book of Isaiah, sitting on a carriage.

"Do you really understand what you are reading?" Philip asked him. "How can I understand if there is nobody to guide me?" the man answered.

He invited Philip to climb onto the carriage. "So Philip spoke to him and, using a passage of Scripture, he announced to him the Good News of Jesus" (Acts 8).

Then he baptised him and the Ethiopian continued his journey, full of joy!

Through baptism, I am a member of the Church and, like the Ethiopian, I need help to know Jesus better. Alone I can do nothing but the Church guides and leads me, she speaks to me of Jesus.

Since my baptism, you live in me, Lord.
Thank you for this wonderful gift!
Make me always more attentive
to your word.
May it always bring me
joy and peace!

St Luke

Luke listened very hard to Mary, Jesus' mother, as she spoke to him about her son: his birth, his childhood, the things he said, his miracles, her joys, her tiredness and her sadness. Mary remembered everything.

So, Luke decided to write all of it down faithfully. He asked the Apostles questions too and carefully checked every detail. He only wrote about what he knew for certain: he did not want to damage Jesus' message, Jesus who is the Truth.

"I have decided, having been carefully informed of everything, to write an account of it" (Luke 1:3).

When I read the Gospel, everything speaks to me of Jesus: I can smell the sheep and the incense, I see Jesus' friends, I hear his words... I only have to shut my eyes: and I feel like I'm there!

Thank you, Luke,
for speaking to us about Jesus.
Thank you for telling us
what he did,
thank you for repeating his words to us.
Your witness builds our faith,
it is faithful to the truth.
With you, we can believe in Jesus,
he who is the Truth.

The martyrs, our elder brothers and sisters in the faith

Jesus was the first martyr, the first to give his life out of love. "There is no greater love than to give your life for your friends" he said (John 15:13).

After Pentecost, many Christians were killed because of their faith. They knew that Jesus had given his life for them, so they gave their life for him.

They loved him so much that they preferred to die rather than betray their faith. They united their sufferings to those of Jesus on the Cross and witnessed to their faith by remaining faithful to the Gospel. How brave!

Today still, in some countries, Christians are persecuted. And I can help them with my prayers.

Lord, I pray for all those
who are thrown into prison,
badly treated or killed
because of their faith.
Give them the courage
to remain faithful until the end.
Give them a sign of your love
and your presence.

St Stephen

Stephen was sure that Jesus was the Son of God and that he was the Messiah, so he said it to everyone he met!

Many listened to him but others were furious. They hurt him and threw stones at him.

Stephen prayed: "Lord Jesus, receive my spirit." He fell onto his knees and cried: "Lord, do not punish them for killing me" (Acts 7:60).

He died forgiving those who killed him, he offered his life for them. He was the first to die out of love for Jesus.

"Pray for your enemies" Jesus told us. It's not an easy thing to do! There are people I don't like much, who annoy me and frighten me.
Stephen gives me the example of true love, a love which always forgives.

Lord,
teach me to forgive
as only you know how to forgive.
Teach me to love
as only you know how to love.

St Tarcisius

Tarcisius was in a hurry. That evening, he was carrying a treasure: the body of Christ. The host was there, sheltered in the hollow of his hand.

Suddenly a gang of boys blocked his path: "What do you have in your hand? A treasure? Show us!"

But Tarcisius did not want them to steal Christ's body and treat it without respect. Despite the blows, he wouldn't open his hand.

The gang ran away and left him dying in the street. His little hand opened only when his friend, who was a priest, found him. Tarcisius was dead. But the host was there, undamaged.

"Go to communion my children! Go to Jesus with love and trust. Go and receive life from him so that you will live for him" (St John Vianney, The Curé d'Ars).

When I receive communion, Jesus gives himself to me, he feeds me and gives me his life.

Lord, I come to you.
My whole body becomes a prayer.
With great respect,
I approach to receive you
in the hollow of my hands,
to receive you in my heart.
Thank you, Lord!

St Blandina

In the town of Lyons in the year 177 forty-eight Christians preferred to die rather than betray their faith. They prayed with all their might.

Among them, a young girl called Blandina encouraged the others. She was weak and small but her faith made her strong. "I am a Christian" she said in front of those who condemned her.

She was sent to be eaten by the animals in the Circus. But guess what happened when the famished beasts entered the arena? It suddenly went quiet and they lay down in front of Blandina! They didn't want to hurt her!

She was killed in another way a few days later, happy to be able to show that she loved Jesus more than anything.

Sometimes I don't dare to say that I am Christian... even though I don't run the risk of being thrown to the lions!

Lord Jesus,
I too am just a child
but I know that you count on me.
Help me when I find it difficult
to remain faithful to you.
Give me your Spirit to live
as a Christian every day.

St Felicity and St Perpetua

On 7th March 303 in the city of Carthage, Felicity and Perpetua, two young mothers, went into the arena hand in hand.
Both of them had been bowled over by the Gospel. United in their love of God, they proclaimed their faith despite the Emperor forbidding them. They were captured and imprisoned but they would never, ever deny Jesus!
"Be firm in the faith" said Perpetua to the Christians who accompanied them.

How they loved each other, these two friends! They threw themselves into each other's arms and kissed each other one last time before dying together in the arena.

My love for Jesus is the same as the love for my brothers and sisters.

You know, Lord
that we can't be Christian on our own!
To love and follow you,
we need others.
To live our faith,
we need the Church.
Help us to remain united with each other
in trust and peace.

The martyrs of Abitina

"Everyone, out!" The Roman centurion burst into a small house where forty-nine Christians were celebrating the Eucharist. He arrested them all and led them to the forum to have them tortured.

Despite their sufferings, they continued to proclaim their faith in Jesus Christ. Young Felix, his friend Saturninus and even little Hilarion, all sang with Tazelita: "Lord Jesus, we are your servants. You are our hope, you are the hope of all Christians. Glory to you, Most Holy God!"

You don't need to be very big, or wise, to love Jesus or to give your life for him. For me, giving my life can simply mean serving those around me.

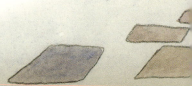

God Most Great, you are our life.
God Most High, you are our strength.
God Most Holy, you are our joy.
God Almighty, you are our hope.
May your name be glorified everywhere!

(The Prayer of the martyrs of Abitina)

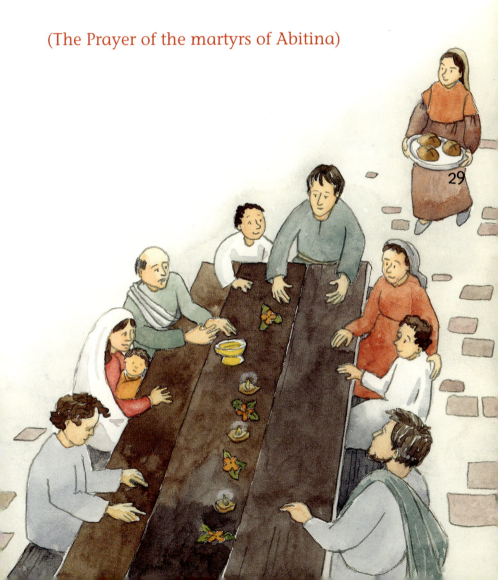

The saints: our friends in heaven

Who are the saints? Are they perfect people? Heroes? Not at all! The saints are ordinary people who loved with an extraordinary love. Who did they love? God, above all. They wanted to do his will, they followed Jesus' path and let themselves be transformed by the Holy Spirit.

They also loved all men and women in the world. In all their different ways of life, they show us all the many ways there are of loving and serving God and other people.

They put into practice the great commandment that Jesus left us: "You will love the Lord your God, with all your heart... and your neighbour as yourself."

Through my baptism, I too am called to holiness. I am called to love and serve. I am called to put myself entirely in God's hands.

Lord Jesus,
all the saints speak to us of you.
They gave you their lives.
They loved you with all their strength.
You call us too to be holy.
Show us the path that leads to you.
Show us the path of holiness.

St Anthony of the Desert

Anthony wanted to be all alone with God. But there was too much noise in the town where he lived. So he went to the desert. There, at least, he could pray, pray and pray again without being disturbed.

In silence and solitude, he listened: God spoke to him and Anthony heard him.
Then he prayed gently: "O God, you are my God, it is you that I seek, my soul thirsts for you" (Psalm 63).

Soon, other men joined him. Following his example, they consecrated their lives to prayer.

My prayers are very important! But to hear what Jesus tells me, I have to be silent and sometimes to switch off the television, the radio and the computer...

I cannot hear you, Lord,
with all this noise!
I cannot see you, Lord
with all this busyness!
So here I am,
I want to be silent
and peacefully
to come to meet you.

St Helen

Who could this grand lady be? It is the Empress Helen! She was very tired after a long journey, all the way from Rome to Jerusalem. She wanted to find Jesus' tomb and pray in the place where he had risen.

After a few days, she found it at last. But what was there, near Calvary, right at the bottom of a well? The cross! The cross on which Jesus was crucified! There was the wood, the nails...

She also found the notice that had been placed above Jesus on the Cross, it proclaimed: "Jesus of Nazareth, King of the Jews" (John 19:19).

Helen forgot her tiredness, she was overwhelmed.

A simple sign of the cross in the morning when I wake up, and a heartfelt sign of the cross in the evening before falling asleep places my life under Jesus' protection.

A stone cross by the side of the road,
a metal cross at the top of the steeple,
a wooden cross beside my bed.
By your cross, O Jesus,
you have given us life.
By your cross, you have given us peace.

St Monica

Monica cried and cried! Her son Augustine was worrying her very much. He was leading a troubled life, very far from Jesus.

Monica was a Christian and wanted Augustine, who was so bright and intelligent, to change his heart and his life. But Augustine didn't seem to want to know about any of this.

Monica often thought of Jesus' words: "Anything you pray for with faith, will be yours" (Matthew 21:22).

So she prayed with all her heart, and all her strength. Would God answer her prayers? Months, years, passed, and then one fine summer day, Augustine suddenly realised how good and great God was. He consecrated all his life to him! Monica's prayer had been answered.

When I pray, God understands me and listens. But do I really believe in the power of prayer?

Lord Jesus,
I have so many things to tell you,
so many things to ask of you…
Sometimes I feel that you don't hear me,
yet I believe that you are there.
Teach me to listen to what you tell me
and to welcome what you give me,
for you alone know what is good for me.

St Augustine

"You do use a lot of quills and parchment!" exclaimed the merchant, as he packed Augustine's purchases.
"So many people ask themselves questions, we simply have to answer them" explained the bishop, smiling. I have to help them to grow in the faith and enlighten their intelligence so that they won't believe what the heretics tell them. I have to defend the Truth."

Yes, it was a big responsibility. Augustine always thought of what Jesus told him: "The man who lives by the Truth comes to the Light" (John 3:21).

So, he prayed and worked so that the Christians would remain faithful to Jesus, who is the Truth.

I too, ask myself questions about God... My intelligence helps me to think, but I do need the Holy Spirit to guide me!

Every day I grow.
Every day I learn new things.
My will is also growing stronger
and my heart gets bigger.
Lord Jesus, make my faith grow
so that I can always believe in you.

St Jerome

What a temper! At his age, he shouldn't get cross like that anymore! For such a holy and wise man, it is really surprising...

There he was tapping his foot: "Ignorant asses! Ignorance of Scripture is ignorance of Christ Himself!"

For twenty years, Jerome had been working hard. Pope Damasus asked him to translate the Bible into Latin so that everyone could read it. What a huge job! He put his knowledge at the service of God's word and the Church that he loved above everything.

Despite my faults, I have many riches and gifts to put at Jesus' service. Being holy isn't the same thing as being perfect!

Sorry, Lord, for the times
when I am bad tempered,
for the times when I am lazy,
for when I am not honest…
I know you love me in spite of it
and that you trust me.
Thank you for the gifts you have given me.
Give me the desire to do things well,
and make an effort to love the Truth.

St Martin

What a freezing winter it was that year!
Martin, a Roman soldier, took pity on a poor beggar who was shivering in the snow. He took out his sword and cut off half his cloak to cover the frozen man. He wanted to give him all of it but he couldn't: the other half, which he kept, belonged to the Roman army.

Later, Martin decided to spend his life praying. As bishop of Tours, he travelled all over Gaul to help people to love Jesus and to spread his Word.

It isn't easy to share, but, every time I do, it is Jesus who I cover with my coat. He said to us: "What you do to one of these little ones who are my friends, you do to me."

Whenever I don't want to give,
whenever I don't want to lend,
whenever I don't want to love,
teach me, Lord, to share,
to be generous and to love those
who need me.

St Nicholas

Everyone was talking about it in Myra: Nicholas, the holy bishop of the town, had just raised three little children from the dead after they had been murdered and hidden in a barrel by an evil innkeeper. What a nightmare!

Nicholas was very good. Through him, God did many miracles. Of course, some extra bits have been added here and there, so now we have a really fine story! But above all, Nicholas gave a witness of a deep faith and great generosity.

Jesus did many miracles. But the Gospel is not just a story! It is the Word of God. Like the disciples, I sometimes doubt. So, with them, I cry out: "Lord, increase our faith" (Luke 17:5).

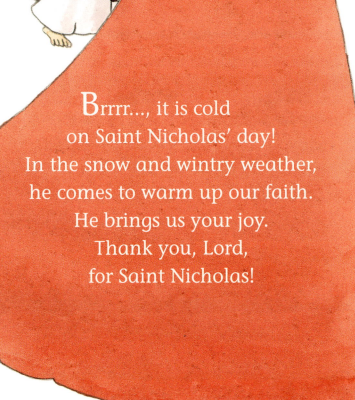

Brrrr..., it is cold
on Saint Nicholas' day!
In the snow and wintry weather,
he comes to warm up our faith.
He brings us your joy.
Thank you, Lord,
for Saint Nicholas!

CTS Children's Books

The Bible for little children, *by Maïte Roche*
(ISBN 1 86082 399 8 CTS Code CH 2)

The Rosary, *by Juliette Levivier*
(ISBN 1 86082 397 1 CTS Code CH 3)

The Way of the Cross, *by Juliette Levivier*
(ISBN 1 86082 398 X CTS Code CH 4)

First prayers for little children, *by Maïte Roche*
(ISBN 978 1 86082 443 2 CTS Code CH 5)

Praying with the friends of Jesus, *by Juliette Levivier*
(ISBN 978 1 86082 444 9 CTS Code CH 6)

Prayers around the Crib, *by Juliette Levivier*
(ISBN 978 1 86082 445 6 CTS Code CH 7)

The most beautiful Christmas Story, *by Maïte Roche*
(ISBN 978 1 86082 446 3 CTS Code CH 8)

Faith for children, *by Christine Pedotti*
(ISBN 978 1 86082 447 0 CTS Code CH 9)

Praying with the first Chritians, *by Juliette Levivier*
(ISBN 978 1 86082 490 6 CTS Code CH 10)

Praying at Mass, *by Juliette Levivier*
(ISBN 978 1 86082 491 3 CTS Code CH 11)

Benedict & Chico, *by Jeanne Perego*
(ISBN 978 1 86082 493 7 CTS Code CH 12)

The beautiful Story of Jesus, *by Maïte Roche*
(ISBN 978 1 86082 492 0 CTS Code CH 13)

Praying with the first Christians: Published 2008 by The Incorporated Catholic Truth Society, 40-46 Harleyford Road, London SE11 5AY. Tel: 020 7640 0042; Fax: 020 7640 0046; www.cts-online.org.uk. Copyright © 2008 The Incorporated Catholic Truth Society in this English-language edition. Translated from the French edition by Geraldine Kay.

ISBN: 978 1 86082 490 6   CTS Code CH 10

Prier avec les premieres chrétiens by Juliette Levivier, illustrations by Anne Gravier, published 2007 by Edifa-Mame, 15-27 rue Moussorgski, 75018 Paris; ISBN Edifa 978-2-9163-5014-1; ISBN Mame 978-2-7289-1221-6. Copyright © Edifa Mame 2007.